First Facts®

OUR GOVERNMENT

THE U.S. SENATE

BY ELLA CANE

CAPSTONE PRESS
a capstone imprint

First Facts are published by Capstone Press,
1710 Roe Crest Drive, North Mankato, Minnesota 56003
www.capstonepub.com

Library of Congress Cataloging-in-Publication Data
Cane, Ella.
The U.S. Senate / by Ella Cane
pages cm. — (First facts. Our government)
 Includes bibliographical references and index.
 Summary: "Informative, engaging text and vivid photos introduce readers to the U.S. Senate"— Provided by publisher.
ISBN 978-1-4765-4202-7 (library binding)
ISBN 978-1-4765-5146-3 (paperback)
ISBN 978-1-4765-5999-5 (ebook PDF)
1. United States. Congress. Senate—Juvenile literature. 2. Legislators—United States—Juvenile literature. 3. Legislation—United States—Juvenile literature. I. Title.
 JK1276.C36 2014
 328.73'071—dc23   2013032209

Editorial Credits
Shelly Lyons, editor; Kyle Grenz, designer; Wanda Winch, media researcher;
Eric Manske, production specialist

Photo Credits
Alamy: EPA/Jonathan Ernst, 9; Courtesy of Army Art Collection, U.S. Army Center of Military History, 21; Getty Images Inc: Alex Wong, 1, Congressional Quarterly/Scott J. Ferrell, 11, 15, CQ Roll Call/Douglas Graham, 17; MCT/Chuck Kennedy, 5; Ed Morita, 13; Newscom: MCT/Dennis Drenner, 19; Shutterstock: Anatoly Tiplyashin, cover (top), atlaspix, cover, 1 (Senate Seal), Mesut Dogan, cover (background); U.S. Senate Photographic Studio, cover (bottom left)

TABLE OF CONTENTS

CHAPTER 1

MAKING THE RULES

Have you and your friends ever had different ideas about something? Did you take a vote to see which idea would win? Then you have done things that happen in the U.S. Senate time and again.

The U.S. Senate is in the legislative branch of the U.S. government. **Senators** make laws for the nation.

senator—a person elected to represent the people in the government; U.S. senators serve in the Senate

Senators gather in the Old Senate chambers in 2006.

CHAPTER 2

BRANCHES OF THE U.S. GOVERNMENT

The legislative branch is one of three parts of the U.S. government. The executive branch and the judicial branch are the other two parts. The executive branch makes sure laws are being followed. The judicial branch explains the U.S. **Constitution** and makes decisions on laws.

In the legislative branch, the House of Representatives and the Senate make up **Congress**. They work together to create laws.

Constitution—the written system of laws in the United States; it states the rights of people and the powers of government

Congress—the elected group of people who make laws for the United States; Congress includes the Senate and the House of Representatives

U.S. GOVERNMENT

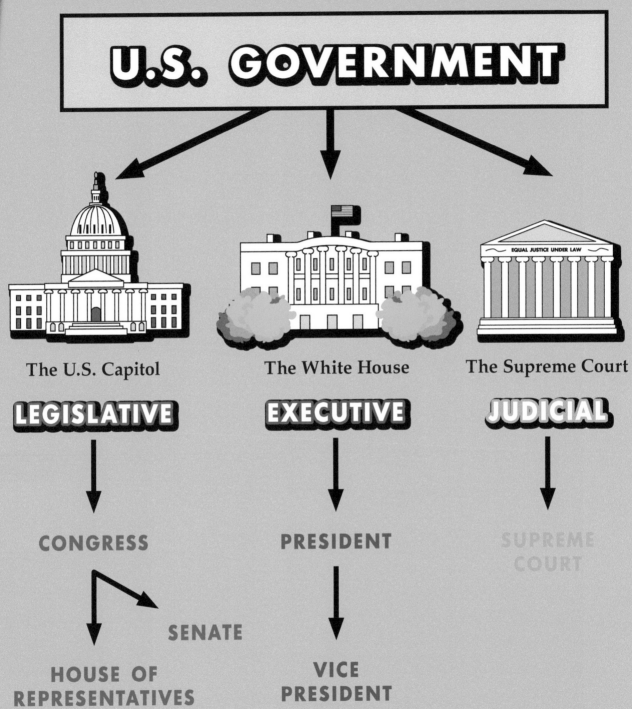

The U.S. Capitol   The White House   The Supreme Court

LEGISLATIVE   **EXECUTIVE**   **JUDICIAL**

CONGRESS   PRESIDENT   SUPREME COURT

SENATE

HOUSE OF REPRESENTATIVES   VICE PRESIDENT

7

CHAPTER 3

A BILL BECOMES LAW

Ideas for new laws can come from anyone. From these ideas, members of Congress write **bills**. Congress members meet and **debate** bills, and then vote. If both the House and the Senate pass a bill, it goes to the president. If the president signs the bill, it becomes law. If the president **vetoes** a bill, it goes back to Congress for another vote. If two-thirds of Congress votes in favor of the bill, it becomes law.

bill—a written idea for a new law
debate—to discuss between two sides with different ways of thinking on a subject; each side tries to convince people that it is right
veto—the power of the president to keep a bill from being approved

President Obama signs a bill in 2013.

CHAPTER 4

WHO CAN BE A SENATOR?

Senators must be at least 30 years old. They also must be U.S. **citizens** for nine years or more. Senators must live in the state in which they are **elected**. Once elected, senators serve for six years. They can run for office as often as they want.

citizen—a member of a country or state who has the right to live there
elect—to choose someone as leader by voting

Senator Roland W. Burris is sworn in as senator of Illinois.

CHAPTER 5

SERVING MANY PEOPLE

The Senate has 100 members. Voters in each state elect two senators. Each senator works for the people of his or her home state. Some senators serve millions of people. For example, the senators of California serve more than 38 million people. But the senators of Wyoming work for fewer than 577,000 people.

FACT Since the first Congress met in 1789, there have been nearly 2,000 U.S. senators.

Senator Mazie Hirono of Hawaii at the State Office of Elections in 2012.

CHAPTER 6

A SENATOR'S JOB

Senators have many duties. They work closely with members of the House of Representatives. Senators and representatives write bills. They also decide how to spend government money. Senators sometimes vote on **treaties**. They also vote on the president's choices for important members of the government.

treaty—a written agreement between countries or groups of people; a treaty is signed by the people's leaders

Senators decide on the president's choice
for a Supreme Court justice.

In addition to their main duties, senators serve on committees. A committee focuses on a certain area, such as **transportation**. Senators also have an office to run. They manage a **staff** and **budget**.

One Senate committee discusses our nation's security.

CHAPTER 7

A SENATOR'S DAY

Senators have busy days. They read new bills and letters from citizens. Senators meet with the president and others to talk about ideas for new laws. Sometimes senators visit with citizens to talk about the country. They also give speeches in Congress meetings and go to important events.

Senator Amy Klobuchar of Minnesota meets with citizens.

CHAPTER 8

THE PRESIDENT OF THE SENATE

The U.S. vice president has a second title. He or she is called the President of the Senate. The President of the Senate votes on a bill only when there is a tie.

FACT The President of the Senate uses a special gavel. It is made of ivory and has no handle. He or she uses the gavel to keep order and to signal when it is time to vote.

Amazing but True!

A senator is supposed to be at least 30 years old, but this rule may have been broken. In 1818 John Henry Eaton was sworn in to the Senate. He was just 28 years old. Perhaps they didn't ask, but he may not have even known his own age. Back then people didn't keep very careful records, and they didn't always know their exact age.

GLOSSARY

bill (BIL)—a written idea for a new law

budget (BUH-juht)—a plan for spending and saving money

citizen (SIT-i-zuhn)—a member of a country or state who has the right to live there

Congress (KON-gress)—the elected group of people who make laws for the United States; Congress includes the Senate and the House of Representatives

Constitution (kahn-stuh-TOO-shun)—the written system of laws in the United States; it states the rights of the people and the powers of government

debate (duh-BATE)—to discuss between two sides with different ways of thinking on a subject; each side tries to convince people that it is right

elect (i-LEKT)—to choose someone as leader by voting

senator (SEN-ah-tur)—a person elected to represent the people in the government; U.S. senators serve in the Senate

staff (STAF)—a group of people who work for the same company or office

transportation (trans-pur-TAY-shun)—a way to move from one place to another

treaty (TREE-tee)—a written agreement between countries or groups of people; a treaty is signed by the people's leaders

veto (VEE-toh)—the power of the president to keep a bill from being approved

READ MORE

Dell, Pamela. *Show Me the U.S. Presidency.* My First Picture Encyclopedias. North Mankato, Minn.: Capstone Press, 2014.

Englar, Mary. *An Illustrated Timeline of U.S. Presidents.* Visual Timelines in History. Mankato, Minn.: Picture Window Books, 2012.

Nelson, Robin, and Sandy Donovan. *The Congress: A Look at the Legislative Branch.* How Does Government Work? Minneapolis: Lerner Publications, 2012.

INTERNET SITES

FactHound offers a safe, fun way to find Internet sites related to this book. All of the sites on FactHound have been researched by our staff.

Here's all you do:

Visit *www.facthound.com*

Type in this code: 9781476542027

Super-cool stuff!

Check out projects, games and lots more at
www.capstonekids.com

INDEX

CRITICAL THINKING USING THE COMMON CORE

1. Senators vote on the president's choices for important members of the government. Why do you think the Senate has that power? (Integration of Knowledge and Ideas)
2. The diagram on page 7 explains the three branches of government. Who is part of the legislative branch? (Key Ideas and Details)